IRVINE

RANCH

different by design

IRVINE

This book is dedicated to all who have participated
in improving the quality of life on the Irvine Ranch.

RANCH

different by design:
images 1960–2000

The Irvine Company, Newport Beach, California

CONTENTS

PREFACE

THE IRVINE RANCH: A LANDOWNER'S PHILOSOPHY

by Donald Bren

This collection of images gives voice to the rich history of the Irvine Ranch. In many ways, it tells the story of one dream unfolding after another has already been set in motion. It is a story of our individual and collective abilities to make these dreams, these visions we have for the places where we live our lives, take shape in the real world. It is my privilege to be part of that process and to be able to share in the pages that follow some of what has taken shape on the ranch over these past forty years.

When I became involved with The Irvine Company in 1977, the master plan that guided and continues to guide the creation of communities on the ranch was already in place. It was an inspired plan, conscious of the relationship people have with the land, thoughtful of the ways we want to live and work, aware of the tremendous forces that shape Southern California. Calling on ideas and sources that we trace back to the great city builders of the past— particularly from those timelessly classic places in the Mediterranean with which we seem to share so much—this master plan is now the subject of serious international study. It is a model for thoughtful urban planning, a testament to both its intellectual dimensions and its pure practicality.

Our particular challenge and opportunity over the years has been to incorporate classic, time-tested architectural, landscaping, and planning forms that honor the spirit and substance of the master plan. It has become our lifework, not only as stewards of the original vision but also as individuals who strive to be sensitive to the ways in which we all wish to live today and tomorrow. Our mission has been to implement this plan and to hold ourselves to the very highest standards in its implementation.

We are all creators of the Irvine Ranch, those of us who live or work or otherwise enjoy our lives here. From residential villages to schools, from the hilltops and canyons to the beaches, from the offices to the shops, we are all participants in the ongoing story of the creation of this wonderful place. And we are all a part of its history.

It is with this realization and with profound personal respect for what has collectively been accomplished that we dedicate this book to all of the people who have played a role, however small, in the improvement of life on the Irvine Ranch. This book is cause for all of us to look back, if even for a few moments, to see the legacy with which we have been entrusted, and rededicate ourselves to the work still ahead.

Donald Bren
Chairman, The Irvine Company

An ounce of farsighted planning is worth a pound of urban
renewal a generation hence.

William Pereira, architect and master planner

INTRODUCTION:

THE LEGACY OF THE IRVINE COMPANY

by Raymond J. Watson

Satellite view of the Southern California coastline, the Irvine Ranch highlighted in orange.

As I leaf through the pages of this beautiful photographic documentation of the transformation of the Irvine Ranch, I reflect back to the summer of 1960.

That was the year I arrived at The Irvine Company headquarters on old Myford Road, a thirty-four-year-old architectural planner reporting for the kind of challenging duty of which dreams are made in my profession. The company had just announced that it would give 1,000 acres in the heart of the ranch for the creation of the University of California's ninth campus. Concurrent with the construction of the University of California, Irvine, the company was committed to the planning and construction of a new town adjacent to the campus.

The idea of a university and a town growing in unison as the central force in the ultimate urbanization of the 93,000-acre ranch was the brainchild of well-known planner and architect William Pereira. I had been attracted to the company by Pereira's vision and The Irvine Company's commitment to it.

By that time, it had become apparent that urban pressures moving south from Los Angeles were not going to bypass the Irvine Ranch. For years there had been speculation only on how, not whether, the company would open up its ranch to development. By 1960, Pereira's vision and the company's commitment to planned, balanced growth were a welcome contrast to the monotonous suburban sprawl that had characterized most of the Los Angeles basin since the end of World War II.

Before long, The Irvine Company, historically known for its ranching and agricultural leadership, was being recognized for its planning and award-winning residential communities and business centers. Over time, the Irvine campus of the University of California was increasingly recognized as one of the finest public research and educational institutions in the country.

So here we are, forty years since William Pereira presented the company with a seventy-four-page plan that suggested a new direction for this great ranch. I, and many others, have spent the better part of four decades implementing this plan. Yet it is important to note that we did not do it alone. After all, community building is not the province of any one company or individual. Communities are built and then held together by their residents, business owners, civic leaders and workers, teachers, and religious institutions. Sometimes a planner,

builder, or employer—but always a neighbor and friend—The Irvine Company has never lost sight of the fact that what it does impacts the lives of many people who live here and share its passion for the land and how it is used.

I believe it has been significantly beneficial to the communities on the ranch that through several owners, The Irvine Company has remained committed to its founding vision. Indeed, as the baton has been handed from one owner to the next, from one elected leader to another, the adoption of the original vision has been not only respected but also endorsed and materially enhanced.

What have I learned over this forty-year experience? It is that successful community planning cannot take place in a vacuum and must reflect current economic, social, and political realities.

Many, many talented and committed people have worked for this great company through the years. They have helped to refine—for the better, I believe—the ideas and vision first advanced in 1960. As one of the earliest pioneers in this grand experiment, I can now say that what has been accomplished on the Irvine Ranch exceeds my wildest expectations.

Read this book and you'll see why.

Raymond J. Watson
First Planner and President, The Irvine Company, 1973–1977

MASTER PLAN:

CREATING A NEW COMMUNITY

Architect and master planner William Pereira in his office with drawings of the University of California's Irvine campus, ca. 1966.

Stretching eight miles along the Pacific coast and twenty-two miles inland, the Irvine Ranch boasts some of the West's most breathtaking scenery and lies at the heart of a region admired for its temperate Mediterranean climate. The ranch is, quite simply, an extraordinary place.

Irvine Company officials were keenly aware of the uniqueness of their holdings as they watched urbanization spread south from Los Angeles County in the late 1950s. As Ray Watson, one of the company's original planners, remarked years later, "The people would have come whether we had planned for their arrival or not. We chose to plan."

As they looked out over this rare expanse of land, Irvine Company planners asked, "What are the possibilities? How will—and how should—people live here? How can we create a habitat for people that is most ideally suited to the development of their full potential?"

The master plan developed for the ranch gave life to a visionary concept: Employment centers would be located near residential villages that offered a wide variety of housing, excellent public schools, parks, and nearby shopping centers. A highly efficient hierarchy of roads would route commuter traffic around, rather than through, residential neighborhoods. Development would be balanced by the permanent preservation of large areas of open space. At the core of the master plan was—and remains—an insistence on balance: a lively interplay between commerce and the arts, between work and leisure, between nature and technology, between private interest and the public good.

In any reflection on the success of the Irvine Ranch master plan, it is important to acknowledge that the plan is not written in stone but is a living document in the purest sense of the term. While the founding principles and spirit of the plan have never changed, certain elements have been modified over the years to reflect the evolving needs and desires of residents of the ranch.

In just forty years, this evolving yet farsighted concept has resulted in what some have referred to as the largest, most successful master-planned urban environment in the United States. It is an achievement that is without precedent.

The vision behind the master plan lives on, and the results are here for everyone to see.

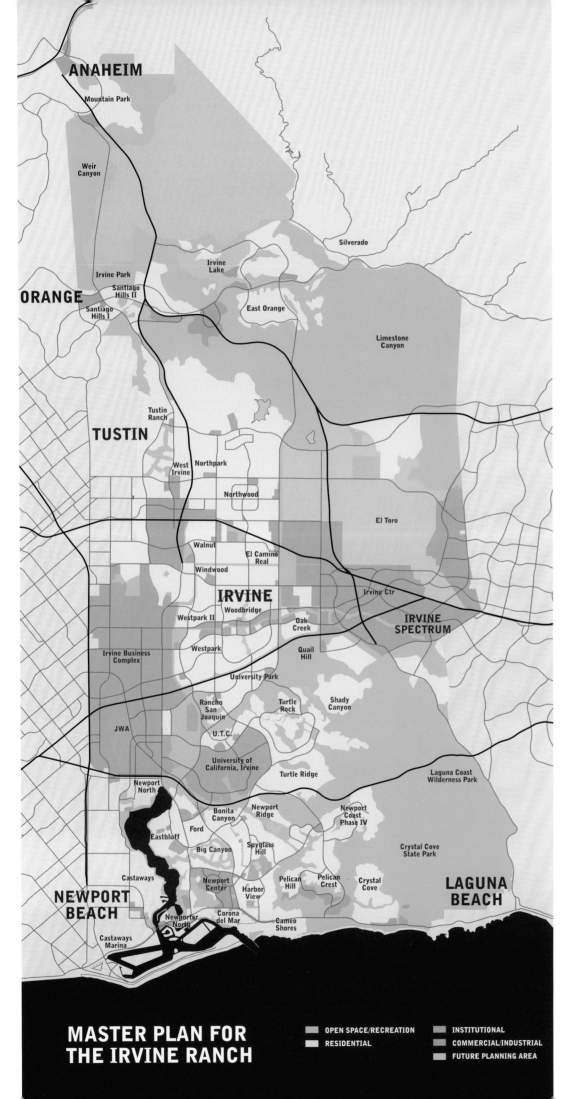

The people would have come whether we had planned for their arrival or not. We chose to plan.

Raymond J. Watson, President, The Irvine Company, 1973–1977

MASTER PLAN FOR THE IRVINE RANCH

- OPEN SPACE/RECREATION
- RESIDENTIAL
- INSTITUTIONAL
- COMMERCIAL/INDUSTRIAL
- FUTURE PLANNING AREA

HISTORY

INDUSTRIAL AND
RESEARCH PARKS

MAJOR EDUCATIONAL INSTITUTIONS
AND CULTURAL OPPORTUNITIES

CAREFULLY PLANNED
RESIDENTIAL COMMUNITIES

THE SIX PART WORLD
OF THE IRVINE RANCH

ABUNDANT
AGRICULTURAL PRODUCTION

WIDE ARRAY OF
RECREATIONAL FACILITIES

DIVERSIFIED COMMERCIAL
CENTERS OF QUALITY

This marketing piece from the 1970s shows how The Irvine Company presented a diversity of land uses to new residents of the ranch.

LOOKING BACK ON THE IRVINE RANCH

There can be no separating a place from its past. Every dream and every decision shows up somewhere, now or in the future, just as our faces show, as time goes by, the lives we are living.

The story of the Irvine Ranch—from Spanish and Mexican ranches, to agricultural dominance, to the high-tech present—is of course part of the larger history of Southern California, carried along by both the romantic restlessness of having to see what's beyond the next hill and the democratic spirit of wanting to make the world a better place. After all, James Irvine, who acquired the property in 1876, was an Irishman who came to San Francisco in the mid-1800s and made his fortune there as a merchant during the California Gold Rush; his heir, known as "J. I.," was a legendary figure in the settlement of the West. These must have been rough-and-ready people, firmly rooted in the here and now.

Yet these landowners and those who have come along since seem always to have kept a keen eye on the future, on what was likely to happen and where things needed to go. The decision in the early 1900s to change the use of the land from ranching to agriculture, replacing flocks of sheep and herds of cows with orange groves and fields of lima beans and corn, was as profound in its own way as the decision forty years ago to bring a University of California campus to the ranch. This close and caring relationship to the land and the effort to consciously consider its most appropriate uses lie at the heart of the Irvine Ranch story.

The Bommer Canyon Cattle Camp was the site of cattle operations on the ranch from the late 1800s to the 1970s.

We rode about a good deal, sometimes coming home in the evening after a thirty- or forty-mile ride pretty thoroughly tired out, but we had to do it in order to see much of the ranch and the flock. We have been making further purchases of land adjoining ours. . . . So there is considerable riding to be done, if one is to see much of it.

James Irvine, after visiting the ranch in summer 1867

Following the San Francisco earthquake in 1906, James Irvine Jr. moved his family from San Francisco to a home on the Irvine Ranch that had originally been built in 1876. The house was destroyed by a fire in 1965.

Cattle roundup,
Bommer Canyon.

Large-scale cattle ranching began on the property in the late 1800s.

Firefighting on the ranch.

Bean threshing machines separated the harvest by grade (ca. 1910). Once the world's largest producer of lima beans, the ranch was forced to sell nearly four thousand acres of bean fields to the U.S. Navy during World War II for the creation of El Toro and Tustin Marine bases.

A solar saltworks once occupied the present site of the Upper Newport Bay Ecological Reserve. Established in 1934, the salt works operated until 1969, when it was destroyed by flood. The Irvine Company donated much of the land to the county for what is now a nature reserve.

Late-summer harvest of tomatoes for processing.

Irvine Ranch farmer cultivates fields.

At their peak in 1967, oranges were harvested from 971,820 orange trees on the ranch. That year, growers on the property shipped one million boxes of oranges, primarily to cities on the East Coast and to Canada.

Cowboy

Tustin Hills Citrus Ass'n
TUSTIN, CALIF.

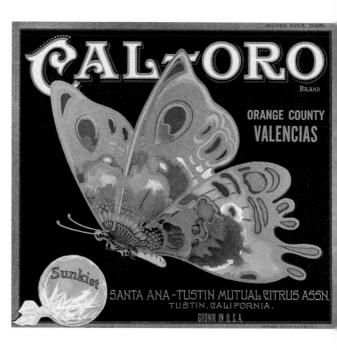

From the 1880s to the 1950s, California citrus growers used thousands of colorful paper labels to identify the boxes of oranges they shipped throughout North America. Orange-crate labels on the Irvine Ranch served as elegant, artistic advertisements for a region that was one of the nation's most productive citrus growers.

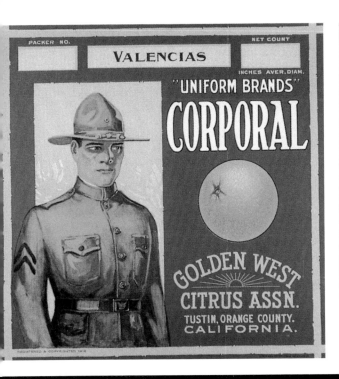

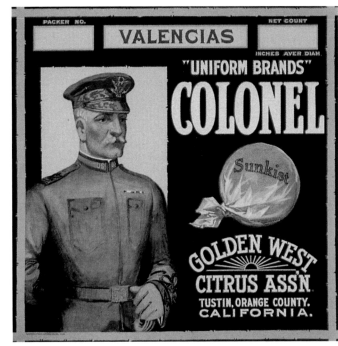

29. JULY. 1917

Employees of The Irvine Company, July 29, 1917.

In spite of the growth of the sugar-beet industry, beans and barley remained the largest of the field crops, and Irvine (James Jr.) took a keen personal interest in their cultivation and harvest, as indeed he did in all of the multitudinous operations of the ranch.

Robert Glass Cleland, author, THE IRVINE RANCH

The general store, still in existence today, was built in 1912, with a post office in the left corner and living quarters upstairs.

Tony Ercegovich, storekeeper, delivers a mail sack to William Cook, postmaster at Irvine, later renamed East Irvine (1963).

The third annual National Boy Scout Jamboree brought fifty thousand Scouts to the ranch in 1953. It was the first international gathering of Scouts in the West and took place in part on what is now known as Fashion Island. The event gave Jamboree Road its name.

Discovered during the construction of the San Joaquin Hills Transportation Corridor, these four-million-year-old remains of a baleen whale are from the Capistrano Formation. The specimen is now on display in the Interpretive Center at Ralph B. Clark Regional Park in Buena Park.

LEISURE

A COMMUNITY AT PLAY

Of all the important choices we make—where we live, how we work—the question of how we choose to spend our free time is the one that perhaps most defines us.

There are as many answers to that question as there are people. To one individual, there may be nothing that makes him feel more fully human than the sight of the ocean at dawn or hearing the crack of the bat at a major-league baseball game. To another person, enjoying a cup of coffee and a newspaper at the corner cafe is the soul's compensation. Some can't live without long walks alone in the wild; others need action, to be around people day and night—museums, restaurants, movies, parties, shopping trips, bright lights.

The truth is that each one of us is a mosaic of many different wants and needs. The more choices there are, and the more access we have to the things that please us, that give our lives meaning, the richer and more complete our lives will be.

Aerial view of
Newport Harbor,
the largest pleasure-
craft harbor in the
United States.

The annual Newport to Ensenada International Yacht Race celebrated its fiftieth year in 1997.

(Above) Newport Harbor.

(Opposite) The Newport to Ensenada International Yacht Race viewed from the coast.

Kayaks at Back Bay.

The seventeenth hole at Pelican Hill's north course.

The result of forty years of planning is an environment where people can spend more time living and less time commuting.

Rob Elliott, Senior Vice President, Urban Planning and Design, The Irvine Company

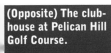

(Opposite) The clubhouse at Pelican Hill Golf Course.

Oak Creek Golf Club in Irvine (above and opposite).

I want open space to be enjoyed, to be used. Oak Creek was the answer for active open space to be utilized by the citizens of Irvine.

Lowell Johnson, Planning Commissioner, 1988

Even though Fashion Island is a high-fashion regional shopping center, it has somehow retained the village character of Newport Beach.

William P. Ficker, author, "The Villages of Newport Beach," NEWPORT BEACH: THE FIRST CENTURY 1888–1988

Fashion Island opened in 1967. After extensive remodeling and landscaping, the center reopened in 1989 with a festive celebration.

The holiday tree at Fashion Island is the tallest real decorated Christmas tree in the nation.

Canary Island
date palms create
dramatic entrances
at Newport Center.

Newport Center serves as Newport Beach's unofficial town center. With more than two hundred retail stores, restaurants, a farmer's market, and movie theaters, Fashion Island is a gathering place for residents and tourists alike.

Neighborhood retail centers have been integrated into residential villages throughout the ranch, providing residents with access to shopping and gathering places. Oak Creek Village Center in Irvine was designed to complement the architecture and landscape of the surrounding community.

(Opposite) Fountains are an important feature of public spaces at Irvine Spectrum Center, establishing the distinctive character of each courtyard.

Irvine Verizon
Amphitheater, a pop-
ular concert venue
(above and opposite).

Irvine Barclay Theatre showcases the performing arts, including contemporary dance, music, and theater. A collaborative venture between the community and the university brought the Barclay to the University of California, Irvine campus in 1990.

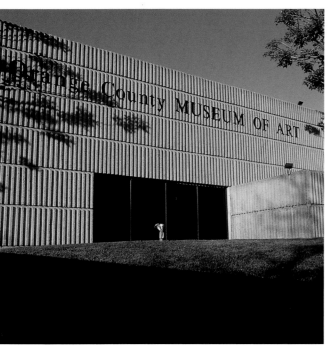

The Orange County Museum of Art in Newport Beach serves Southern California with a rich variety of exhibitions and programs and brings a dynamic spark to the cultural life of the entire community.

Our kids have a neighborhood street, probably with as strong an identity as I grew up on. The kids can walk to school. They have friends who can walk over. We're within a stone's throw of the boys' and girls' clubs, and they can play on a hardwood basketball court. We have a dozen tennis courts within three or four blocks. There's a lagoon you can go sailing on.

David Price, ORANGE COUNTY REGISTER

A bike path in Woodbridge provides a link to the regional trail system that runs throughout the Irvine Ranch.

There are still places on the ranch where you can hike all day and hardly see a soul. As the world grows up around us, our open spaces—the lands left wild or made into places that encourage us to slow down a little and play—call out for us to come to them more than they ever have before.

Marci Manther, resident of the village of Woodbridge.

Irvine Regional Park, the first park on the Irvine Ranch, was dedicated to Orange County by The Irvine Company in 1897.

Pool, landscaping, and fireplace create a resort atmosphere at the Four Seasons Hotel in Newport Center (right and opposite).

The use of landscaping is central to the creation and reinforce-
ment of outdoor spaces in our communities. The landscape
design must have a strong, clear spatial and thematic concept,
which works with and is responsive to the site and the
architecture. Collectively, they give each community unique
and deliberate character.

Rob Elliott, Senior Vice President, Urban Planning and Design, The Irvine Company

A city is much more than sound planning and architectural integrity. Its character is defined by its residents. Irvine's greatness today reflects the countless contributions, large and small, of people over the years who have chosen to live here, work here, play here, and operate a business in Irvine. Throughout the city's history, our company has worked in partnership with community leaders and individual residents whose big dreams and ambitious standards have made Irvine—and keep Irvine—one of the best places to live in America.

Donald Bren, Chairman, The Irvine Company

The bright lights of Irvine Spectrum Center attract millions of visitors every year.

Myrtles Court at
Irvine Spectrum
Center.

Gibraltar City Gate at Irvine Spectrum Center is one of three distinctive gates marking each entrance to the center.

The design of the courtyards at Irvine Spectrum Center was influenced by architecture at the Alhambra, the palace of the Moorish kings, in Granada, Spain.

Summer Concert
Series at Irvine
Spectrum Center.

The Dorado Court
Tower at Irvine
Spectrum Center.

Bold architecture, strong landscaping, and dynamic public spaces tie together The Market Place, a major regional shopping center bisected by several roadways (left and opposite).

The monumentalization of the most common elements, the use of colors and textures that are unusual but still connected with the surrounding territory, the recognition of scale and the simplicity of the architectural designs have contributed to the success of [The Market Place].

LOTUS 89 ARCHITECTURAL REVIEW

As skilled master planners and business managers, we strive to build and enhance the working and living environments that enrich life in our communities. With a long-term focus, we are proud to design and build attractive residential communities and business properties that withstand the test of time.

Donald Bren, Chairman, The Irvine Company

A sunset jog on the jetty in Corona del Mar.

WORK

WORKING ENVIRONMENTS

The Irvine Ranch has always been a good place to work, whether one was herding cattle and sleeping under the stars in the late 1800s or "in conference" with a client in the boardroom in the late twentieth century.

The ranch is one of the nation's most vibrant and diverse regional economies, with some 250,000 employed. There is an entrepreneurial spirit on the ranch and an energy that sparks all sorts of opportunities. If Orange County were a nation, it would be one of the top thirty countries in the world in terms of gross domestic product, ahead of Argentina, Austria, and Denmark. This is still very much a working ranch.

People work hard here. They always have and they probably always will. One reason is that they like the balance that surrounds them. When planning the working environments on the ranch, The Irvine Company was guided by two major considerations: One was the idea that if people could live near their work, they would have fuller, more productive lives. The other was that the workplace should aspire to provide not only a comfortable environment but also a beautiful one. When we like where we work and are inspired by our surroundings, we work harder and smarter.

These ideas seem to be paying off. And it's all right that, from time to time, we have moments when we wonder how any work gets done at all.

Anyone who has strolled through Newport Center . . . cannot fail to be impressed by the attention paid by its designers to aesthetic and psychological factors.

Alvin Toffler, FUTURE SHOCK, 1970

500 Newport Center Drive
Newport Beach, CA 92660

Lobby of The Irvine
Company offices,
Newport Center.

Moonrise over
Newport Center, only
a quarter mile from
Newport Bay.

Newport Center attracts companies seeking office space close to good neighborhoods and world-class recreational facilities.

The Irvine Company is indefatigably planning and building spaces for working and living in the best of all possible worlds. A new and marvelous setting where the beauty of the natural landscape forms a backdrop to subtly impressive office complexes, residential communities in the garden-city style, an important university, and gigantic shopping centers.

LOTUS 89 ARCHITECTURAL REVIEW

The master plan for Newport Center, which began in 1965, envisioned a balance of housing, jobs, cultural amenities, recreation, and open space within one six-hundred-acre environment. Today it is one of the nation's most successful mixed-use centers (right and opposite).

It's the world's best-kept secret in terms of opportunity. Of all the developments I've seen in the U.S., Irvine Spectrum is the most impressive.

John Dean, CEO of Silicon Valley Bank, THE WALL STREET JOURNAL, January 14, 1998

Spacious, landscaped pedestrian walkways are an integral part of working environments on the ranch.

Some 2,600 companies, employing 55,000 people, are located in Irvine Spectrum, which has core industry clusters in computer hardware, software, automotive, biotechnology, and medicine.

The strength of the landscape design in Irvine Spectrum is in its simplicity. Slopes, hedges, evergreen trees, and palms create a framework and context for the buildings. The timeless architecture of the structures reinforces the identity of the broader research park that has been created by the landscape.

Rob Elliott, Senior Vice President, Urban Planning and Design, The Irvine Company

The 5,000-acre Spectrum, which sits in the heart of Orange County . . . is one of America's most successful business parks, outdoing such rivals as North Carolina's Research Triangle in everything from office space to employees.

THE ECONOMIST, July 18–24, 1998

Nikken's state-of-the-art U.S. corporate headquarters in Irvine. Nikken is a leading supplier of wellness products and one of the largest network marketing companies in the world.

A view of one of
Irvine's major busi-
ness districts from
the San Joaquin
Wildlife Sanctuary in
the heart of the city.

Towers of gleaming travertine marble set along an expansive palm-lined promenade. Located at the intersection of the 405 freeway and Jamboree Road, Jamboree Center is an Orange County landmark and home to some of the area's leading companies (left).

Palms mark the entryways at Jamboree Center in Irvine (left) and MacArthur Court in Newport Beach (above).

The signature of this and other commercial centers on the Irvine Ranch is timeless architecture and a consistent landscaping palette.

MacArthur Court, near John Wayne Airport.

Mature trees and carefully planned landscapes complement office architecture and give commercial centers their character.

The Irvine Ranch is a place where a lot of people, professionals and volunteers, are working very hard to make a good future possible.

Frank C. McGee, Editor, NEW WORLDS MAGAZINE and author, UCI: THE FIRST 25 YEARS

Offices for the law firm of Brobeck & Phleger. Companies serving high-technology industries are moving into campus-like settings to be near their clients.

Each job center has become a well-known business address in Orange County, where growing companies, large and small, provide employment and attract other businesses seeking a planned environment.

Residents of Irvine voted to become a city in 1971. The Civic Center, (above and right), is one of twelve facilities maintained by the city and available for public use.

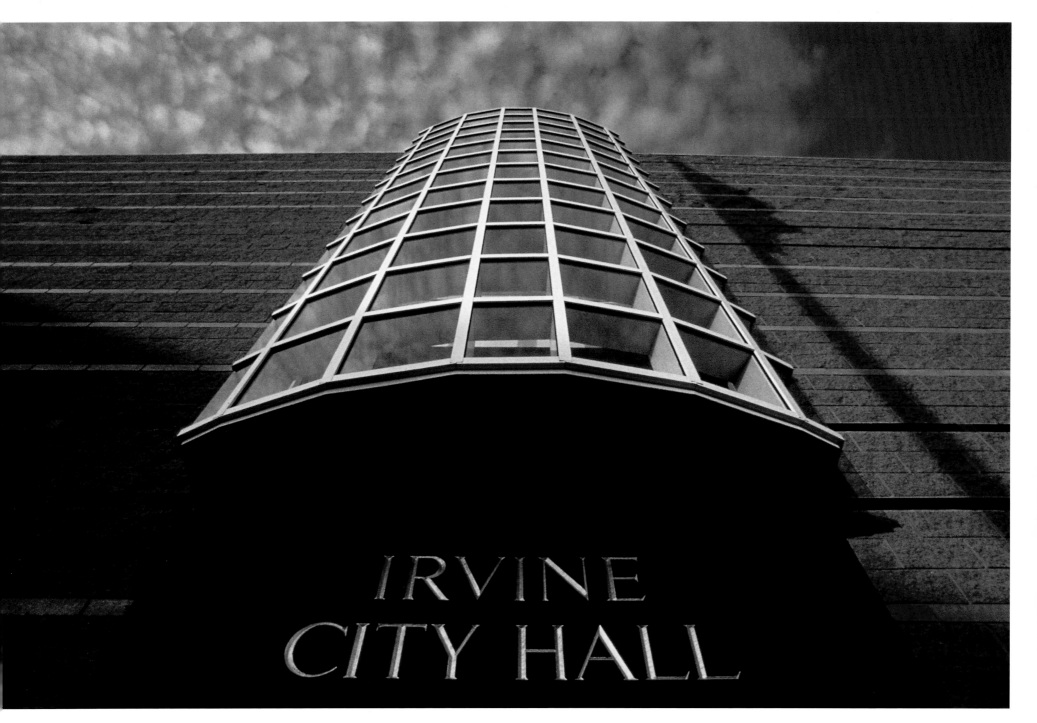

IRVINE
CITY HALL

As Irvine has matured following the thoughtful, deliberate, and comprehensive master plan for its completion, the city continues to earn international attention and acclaim as perhaps the largest, most successful master-planned city anywhere. The ultimate compliment is paid: Irvine is a city that works.

Donald Bren, Chairman, The Irvine Company

Irvine is not designed as an isolated new town. We recognize it as part of the Southern California metropolitan fabric. Roads, transit systems, utilities, regional parks, and major educational institutions must be compatible with, and contribute to, the needs of neighboring cities.

Raymond J. Watson, President, The Irvine Company, 1973–1977

John Wayne Airport is a part of the regional transportation system and provides access to cities throughout the United States.

(Opposite) Toll booths on San Joaquin Hills Transportation Corridor, which bisects the southern portion of the ranch.

(Opposite and right) Views of the interior of John Wayne Airport, also referred to as the Santa Ana or Orange County Airport.

The impressive realizations about the Beckman Laser Institute are that it is a totally integrated university/community endeavor and that its programs are comprehensive. From research to clinical practice to veterinary treatment, the scope, breadth, and quality of its programs are unrivalled. It is truly a world center.

Frederick M. Grazer, M.D., F.A.C.S.

The Arnold and Mabel Beckman Center of the National Academy of Sciences and Engineering was built on the University of California, Irvine campus to provide a focal point for the scientific community of the West.

Outdoor spaces at Irvine Spectrum, University Research Park, and Irvine Technology Center provide places for collaboration and interaction.

The real question is: How do you balance growth with preservation of the beautiful natural environment? As open space lands are set aside, it actually makes the entire community more valuable.

Larry Agran, Mayor of Irvine

HOME

VILLAGES OF THE IRVINE RANCH

The Irvine Company's first architect and planner, Ray Watson, has described the villages of the Irvine Ranch as a series of pearls, each special in its own way. Some have strong central recreational features, such as the lake at Woodbridge or the open-space paseo at Harbor View. Others, such as Eastbluff, feature schools and shopping in the heart of the village. Turtle Rock and Northpark are defined by distinct natural features. As Watson has noted, it is not until all of these pearls are strung together that one begins to see the beauty of the necklace that represents the residential villages planned and created on the Irvine Ranch.

The Irvine Company's current planners and architects spend nearly as much time looking back on the villages created over the past forty years as they do looking forward to the communities that remain to be built. Figuring out what worked, what did not, and how to incorporate those lessons to improve the way people will live their lives tomorrow is a task taken very seriously.

Ask a ranch resident where he or she lives and you won't likely hear "Irvine." Instead, you'll hear the names of the villages that designers and planners have come from around the world to see and study—names like Northwood and University Town Center, Oak Creek and Westpark. This has been the true measure of success in community planning: creating a place where people feel their homes extend beyond the front door and into the neighborhoods in which they live.

The Irvine Company will devote its energies to making certain that all elements of the new city—from signs to landscaping to types of buildings—conform to aesthetic standards that assure an attractive environment. Our vast land holdings compel our meeting this responsibility.

William R. Mason, President, The Irvine Company, 1966–1973

The distinctive character of each village is enhanced by the quality of building materials used and by carefully planned entrances that create a sense of arrival and reinforce the personalities of these unique neighborhoods.

Landscaping thrives in the climate of coastal Orange County. The region shares its climate with three other parts of the world—the Mediterranean and small sections of the South African and Australian coasts.

Entry markers in Newport Coast incorporate beautiful stonework and mature landscaping (left and opposite).

Luxurious homes at Pelican Hill and Pelican Point are neighbors to the golf course and the coast.

Custom-built homes along the coast reflect the architectural styles of Italy, southern France, and Spain and are characterized by the use of forms and materials that work with the hillside terrain and provide relief from the sun.

Our main challenge in planning the ranch was to create a community we all could be proud of.

Raymond J. Watson, President, The Irvine Company, 1973–1977

Our company's commitment to the Irvine Ranch master plan is long term. Our goal and mission is to continue planning imaginative new communities in a way that serves the people who have come to this special place and share our vision. With each passing day, the ranch is a better place to live. I passionately believe over time it will only get better.

Rob Elliott, Senior Vice President, Urban Planning and Design, The Irvine Company

Crystal Cove was in the planning stages for thirty-seven years before ground was broken in the year 2000 (this page and opposite).

I have lived abroad and have visited many foreign cities and appreciate the arts, architecture, academic life, and all the other amenities the good life has to offer. I choose to live here because it provides me with all of this in a beautiful setting with a wonderful climate.

W. F. Rylaarsdam in a letter to the editor, LOS ANGELES TIMES

The Castaways
community in the
Back Bay area of
Newport Beach.

The village of Northwood in Irvine is located at the base of hills leading into the northern stretches of the Irvine Ranch.

Pereira's plan was widely regarded as visionary. He designed
self-contained communities, complete with shopping centers,
parks, and greenbelts—a far cry from the aimless suburban
sprawl that had been spilling over into Orange County as Los
Angeles spread to the south.

FORTUNE magazine, December 1976

A golf course serves
as the primary focal
point and major
recreational feature
in Tustin Ranch
(opposite).

Villa Siena (right) and Newport Bluffs apartment communities (above) offer rental housing alternatives on the ranch.

Open space and natural landforms give the village of Turtle Rock its physical character.

A central open space paseo and garden park system connect neighborhoods in the village of Northpark.

(Above) This unusual circular park in Harvard Square serves as the focal point of the enclave, located within the village of Walnut.

Entry marker at the village of Oak Creek in Irvine.

174

Fifty-year-old eucalyptus trees, planted to protect crops from the Santa Ana winds, were preserved in the village of Northpark.

Architectural detail is
an important feature
of the village of
Northpark in Irvine.

Irvine Cove (in the foreground) on the southern edge of the ranch. Laguna Beach can be seen in the distance.

More than 25,000 people live in Wood-bridge, Irvine's largest village.

With its own recreation, schools, business centers, and a variety of housing styles, Woodbridge is perhaps Irvine's most acclaimed village.

The public reaction to the opening of Woodbridge in 1976 was overwhelming. Ten thousand people showed up for the opportunity to buy 350 homes. It really hit home for me just how eager Southern Californians were for an alternative to unplanned subdivisions.

Raymond J. Watson, President, The Irvine Company, 1973–1977

Linda Isle, a partially submerged sandbar, lower left, served as the sands in THE SANDS OF IWO JIMA starring John Wayne, a local resident. After nine years of planning, The Irvine Company dredged half a million cubic yards of sand and silt to create the island's lagoon in 1967.

Homes along Newport Harbor, with Promontory Point apartment community in the background.

EDUCATION

EXCELLENCE IN LEARNING

What gives a community hope that it will be a better place tomorrow than it is today? Buildings, neighborhoods, open space, physical infrastructure—these are important tools to the community builder. But ultimately, it is the strength of the education system and the children who will call these places home in the ensuing decades that will determine success or failure.

A similar realization by The Irvine Company and the Board of Regents of the University of California in 1960 led to an unlikely agreement to locate the ninth campus of the University of California system on the Irvine Ranch. This decision ushered in a new era for the ranch.

What struck many as experimental at that time—the company's commitment to designing a new town around the campus of the University of California, Irvine—has had far-reaching consequences that go beyond the university or the city of Irvine.

Through the years, the relationship between the company and the much larger educational mandate of the area has deepened. Community colleges and K-12, public and private, are all part of the educational fabric of the Irvine Ranch, and these institutions are consistently ranked among the finest in the state. People move to the ranch for the schools. This excellence in education is a testament to the quality of teachers, administration, and faculty on the ranch and to the great pride the community takes in its schools.

Clark Kerr [President of the University of California, Irvine] drew out on a piece of yellow paper the idea of a circle with disciplines around it. We then picked up on the idea and elaborated on what would be distributed around the core.

Daniel G. Aldrich Jr., first Chancellor, University of California, Irvine

Hired by the University of California to find a home for a new campus, Pereira recommended a site on the Irvine Ranch. In 1960, The Irvine Company donated one thousand acres to the university. In the early stages of construction (above), cement was poured for the foundation.

In November 1965, workers plant a large tree near the university library. The campus commons is in the background.

Aerial view of the campus to the south-west, shortly before dedication of the University of California, Irvine on June 26, 1964.

We were no longer an agrarian society, yet we would be on the site of a great agricultural landscape. In essence, the first encroachment of people would be those coming to build a university. And the university might use as its lab the community that would develop around it. The chance to relate the ideas of research, scholarship, and teaching to the needs of society seemed like an unparalleled opportunity.

Daniel G. Aldrich Jr., first Chancellor, University of California, Irvine

On June 26, 1964, President Lyndon Johnson spoke before an audience of 15,000 at the dedication of the campus of the University of California, Irvine. Other dignitaries on hand included California Governor Pat Brown and UC Irvine President Clark Kerr. President Johnson arrived by helicopter. Everyone else drove in on a single two-lane road.

Behind a field of daffodils, a view of the Science Lecture Hall (left) and Steinhaus Hall (right), formerly called the Natural Science Building.

A site on the Irvine Ranch [for a new University of California campus] held many potential benefits, the principal of which was the chance to plan the area around the campus as a true university-community development. Single ownership of the land made such planning a possibility.

Daniel G. Aldrich Jr., first Chancellor, University of California, Irvine

From the terrace of the Main Library, a view of Humanities Hall (left) and Murray Krieger Hall (right), formerly known as the Humanities Office Building.

Fence and sign at the early entrance to the University of California, Irvine property are reminiscent of the site's ranch history.

Pereira envisioned a university directly linked with a city.

Frank C. McGee, Editor, NEW WORLDS magazine and author, UCI: THE FIRST 25 YEARS

An architectural bridge links the School of the Arts to the School of the Humanities.

Biological Sciences II, University of California, Irvine.

Reines Hall, University of California, Irvine.

From left to right, Physical Sciences Research Facility, Rowland Hall, Physical Sciences Lecture Hall and Classroom Building, and Reines Hall, University of California, Irvine.

202

Student Center,
University of
California, Irvine.
In the distance is the
Main Library.

Founded in 1979 as the northern satellite campus of Saddleback College, Irvine Valley College became an independent college and was renamed in 1985.

With 11,000 students, Irvine Valley College boasts one of the highest percentages of students who transfer to four-year institutions.

The whole economy is better when you have better schools.
Orange County is starting to realize that when you make an
investment [in education], the returns are substantial.

Bill Habermehl, Associate Superintendent, Orange County Department of Education,
LOS ANGELES TIMES, September 7, 2000

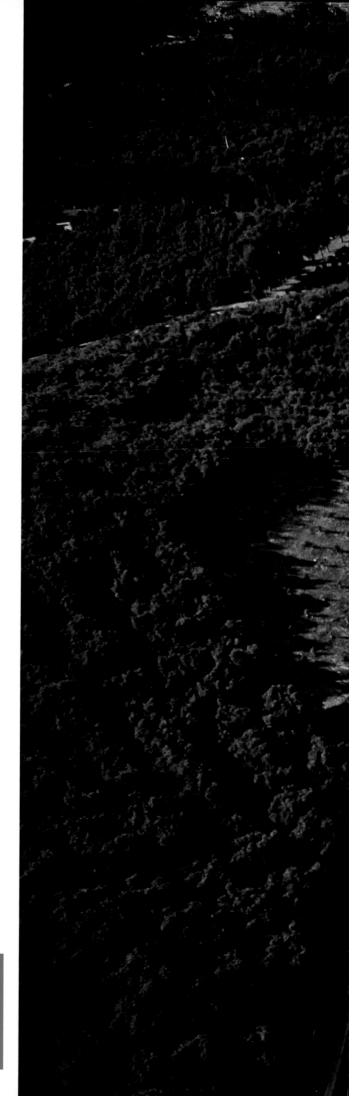

Northwood High
School in the Irvine
Unified School
District.

Northwood High
School.

The award-winning Irvine Unified School District was rated by a Harvard University study as one of the top three school systems in the nation.

Irvine public schools enjoy a broad curriculum with an emphasis on technology, science, health, and the fine arts.

All five school districts serving the Irvine Ranch—Irvine, Laguna Beach, Newport-Mesa, Orange, and Tustin—have earned a reputation for quality at every level.

Sage Hill School
(above and opposite),
an independent non-
denominational school
on the Irvine Ranch.

Sage Hill School offers a dynamic learning environment, small classes, a strong arts curriculum, and state-of-the-art technology facilities.

Given Irvine residents' close proximity to schools, students often arrive for class on bicycles.

The Newport Beach Public Library's central campus on Avocado Avenue (above) and three other campuses throughout the city pride themselves on being at the cultural, educational, and informational heart of Newport Beach.

CONSERVATION

Bommer Canyon is part of the 39,000 acres on the ranch that are set aside as permanent open space. In accordance with the 1988 Open Space Agreement passed by Irvine voters, Bommer Canyon will be given to the city at no cost.

AN ABIDING COMMITMENT TO THE LAND

It is said that the early cattle hands gave special names to the places they loved on the ranch. There was "top of the world" on a hilltop in Shady Canyon, the "willow pond" in the northern foothills, and Irvine Cove on the beach near Laguna. These are the places they would go to escape from the rest of the world.

While the reasons people give to "get away from it all" have changed dramatically over the last hundred years, the fact that you can still find these places in their natural settings has not. The wildlands on the Irvine Ranch remain, in part, because planning balanced communities requires the preservation of large areas of undisturbed land for plants and animals to live and for people to enjoy.

The Irvine Company's master plan for the ranch envisions nearly 39,000 acres of the original ranch preserved as open space, much of it to be deeded to public ownership. Largely through a partnership between the company and the Nature Conservancy, the open space is actively being managed to improve habitat value and facilitate public access.

Laguna Coast, Limestone Canyon, Crystal Cove, Quail Hill, Bommer Canyon—these are just a few of the places that will never be disturbed or developed. If you live on the ranch, the chances are good that one of these places is not far from your front door.

We are in a very different time than that in which the first Irvine Ranch cattle hands lived, but we still have the need to feel the same cool breezes that touch the ridge tops, or to see deer scampering up the side of a mountain. Most people say they need these places now more than ever.

The 1988 Open Space Agreement ensures that nearly one thousand acres of Shady Canyon will be permanently preserved as open space.

The federal government has a wonderful national parks system, but Yellowstone isn't just down the road. These magnificent lands are. The Open Space Agreement is a vision come true for Orange County and what it means is that people who come to this county are going to have the values that drew them here in the first place.

Bruce Babitt, United States Secretary of the Interior, 1993-2000

Limestone Creek is part of Limestone Canyon, a designated wilderness area.

The "Sinks" in Limestone Canyon originated some thirty-five million years ago when the sea floor suddenly thrust upward. Centuries of erosion have created the look of a miniature Grand Canyon.

Aerial view of ridges above Shady Canyon.

The approach to open space preservation on the Irvine
Ranch is something to be admired by other cities and states.
I encourage residents to come out here at least once to
experience the natural beauty that the ranch has to offer.

Trish Smith, Nature Conservancy, Director of Open Space Reserve

The hills of the northern section of the Irvine Ranch looking toward the Cleveland National Forest.

Our greatest legacy is the preservation of diverse landscapes like those we see around us today.

Steve McCormick, Director, Nature Conservancy, ORANGE COUNTY REGISTER, August 7, 1992

Orange monkey flower.

Indian paintbrush.

Wild hyacinth.

Arroyo lupine.

Parry's phacelia.

Parry's phacelia.

Chalk liveforever.

Indian paintbrush.

California polypody.

California everlasting.

Milk thistle.

Datura, also known as jimson weed.

Lemonadeberry.

Branching phacelia.

Fuschia-flowered gooseberry.

Coastal prickly pear.

Dove weed.

Sugarbush.

Long-stemmed buckwheat.

Yucca.

Arroyo lupine (left).

A view of a reservoir from the village of Turtle Rock in Irvine, with Shady Canyon in the distance.

Irvine Lake, now a major recreational area, was created by The Irvine Company on the northern ranch in the 1930s. The reservoir enabled agriculture to flourish on previously arid land. The creation of water systems throughout the ranch—canals connecting reservoirs to the flat lands—allowed row crops and the citrus industry to boom.

For the first time, the Nature Conservancy is working with private lands to manage them for the landowner as a nature preserve. It is truly a unique venture.

Steve McCormick, Director, Nature Conservancy

Laguna Coast Wilderness Park was designated in part to protect threatened animal and plant species.

These lands are extremely important for preservation because they support some of the greatest and most valuable and diverse wildlife habitat in Southern California. The Irvine Company has made the commitment to bring an organization like the Nature Conservancy in to manage these lands for their habitat values, so that by the time they come into public ownership, the value of these lands in terms of resource protection and value to wildlife and plants will be that much better.

Trish Smith, Nature Conservancy, Director of Open Space Reserve

Gray-bird grasshopper.

Diamondback rattlesnake.

Coyote.

Great blue heron.

Sara Orangetip butterfly.

Cactus wren.

Master planning is a matter of determining not only what is built upon the land, but what is not.

William Pereira, architect and master planner

Muddy Canyon's mile-long wildlife corridor links Crystal Cove State Park with the coastal canyons.

In the late 1970s, The Irvine Company transferred ownership of coastal lands to the state of California for the creation of Crystal Cove State Park.

From the beginning, our primary challenge was to keep the coast from being subdivided. What resulted from years of planning was the preservation of seventy-eight percent of the Newport Coast as open space.

Raymond J. Watson, President, The Irvine Company, 1973–1977

Thanks to a truly collaborative effort including the hard work of scientists, engineers, committed individuals, and organizations, the San Joaquin Marsh is once again a vital habitat for fish and birds.

Mary Nichols, Secretary of the California Resources Agency

The San Joaquin Wildlife Sanctuary, in the heart of the city of Irvine, is the largest coastal freshwater marsh in Southern California and a major stopover site for some two hundred species of migratory birds.

At right, great blue heron.

Turkey vulture.

Baby hummingbirds.

Black-crowned night heron juvenile.

Black-necked stilt.

262

Red-tailed hawks.

Dove eggs.

Vegetation in Emerald Canyon showed the regenerative power of nature in the years following the 1993 Laguna Beach wildfires. The recovery of plant species in coastal sage scrub and grassland was amazingly quick. These pictures (above and opposite, left to right) were taken from 1991 to 1997, beginning with an image at top left taken before the fires.

In the 1988 Open Space Agreement, the voters of Irvine identified special natural features to be preserved, such as ridgelines and canyons. Under the agreement, whenever The Irvine Company builds in a designated area, the company gives a corresponding parcel of open space to the city.

The idea of shifting long-planned development away from ecologically fragile or culturally important open space was, at first, very controversial. In the end, however, all understood that we had a rare opportunity to make an important and lasting contribution to our community.

Ray Catalano, planner, former Irvine city councilman

In accordance with the 1988 Open Space Agreement, more than six hundred acres of the Quail Hill area will belong to the City of Irvine.

IRVINE RANCH CHRONOLOGY

1864   James Irvine and partners purchase the 50,000-acre Rancho San Joaquin from Jose Sepulveda.

1865   James Irvine and partners purchase 50,000-acre Rancho Lomas de Santiago from William Wolfskill.

1876   James Irvine buys out partners to form Irvine Ranch at southern edge of Los Angeles County.

1886   James Irvine dies. Ranch left in trust to his son, James "J.I." Irvine Jr.

1889   Orange County formed out of what was part of Los Angeles County.

1893   James Irvine Jr. assumes full control of Irvine Ranch at the age of 25.

1894   The Irvine Company is formed. James Irvine Jr. makes the company the owner and operator of the Irvine Ranch.

1897   The Irvine Company donates 160 acres to create Irvine Regional Park.

1904   The company sells 400 acres of what would later become Corona del Mar. Proceeds help finance water infrastructure for agricultural improvements.

1937   James Irvine Jr. establishes James Irvine Foundation for purpose of supporting educational and charitable institutions in California.

1942   U.S. government acquires land from the company for El Toro and Tustin Marine Air Bases.

1947   James Irvine Jr. dies. James Irvine Foundation inherits majority of company stock. Myford Irvine, son of James Irvine Jr., becomes president of the company and chairman of the foundation.

1953   Irvine Ranch hosts 50,000 Boy Scouts at International Boy Scout Jamboree.

1957   University of California begins search for new campus site. Search focuses on area south of University of California, Los Angeles.

1959	Myford Irvine dies.
1960	New era for Irvine Ranch begins when The Irvine Company donates 1,000 acres to the University of California for a new campus. Company also announces its intent to plan and build a new town adjacent to the campus.
	Orange County is the fastest growing county in the United States.
	The Irvine Company begins master plan to guide all future development on the ranch.
1964	Village of Eastbluff, the first residential village on the ranch, opens with variety of housing, connecting greenbelts, schools, and shopping.
	County Supervisors adopt master plan for first phase of Irvine Ranch.
1965	University of California, Irvine campus opens.
1967	Fashion Island opens, first regional retail center on Irvine Ranch. Shopping center becomes focal point in mixed-use Newport Center.
1971	With a population of 20,000, residents of Irvine vote by a two-to-one margin to become a city.
1976	Forced by changes in federal tax laws to sell its majority interest in the Irvine Ranch, the James Irvine Foundation seeks a buyer for the property.
1977	Irvine Foundation sells The Irvine Company to new investors.
1983	Population of city of Irvine reaches 75,000.
	Donald Bren becomes majority shareholder of Irvine Ranch.
	Irvine Spectrum grows to 5,000-acre research park and becomes major employment center with opening of Alton freeway interchange.
1988	Citizens of Irvine approve Irvine Open Space Agreement with The Irvine Company.
1989	Newport Coast community begins.
1992	The Irvine Company Open Space Reserve is created on Irvine Ranch. Company retains the Nature Conservancy to plan and manage reserve.
1996	Irvine Spectrum Center opens.
	New university-related research park opens adjacent to University of California, Irvine campus to encourage collaboration between business and academia.
1997	University of California Regents and The Irvine Company reach agreement to expand University Research Park onto University of California, Irvine campus.
1999	Irvine Company donates land along the coast to county, tripling the size of Laguna Coast Wilderness Park.
2000	Population of Irvine Ranch reaches 200,000. Number of people working on the ranch reaches 250,000.

ACKNOWLEDGMENTS

Proceeds from the sale of this book will be used to fund the enhancement of existing natural resources on lands designated for permanent preservation on the Irvine Ranch.

ISBN 0-9709085-0-4

Produced and edited by Garrett White and Karen Hansgen, Los Angeles, CA
Book and jacket design by Simon Johnston @ praxis:
Assistant designer: Annabelle Gould
Printed by Gardner Lithograph, Buena Park, CA

The editors would like to thank the many current and former employees of The Irvine Company who participated in the production of this book. Thanks also to Martha Cook; Mary Daily; Nancy Francis; David Gardner, Kevin Regan, and Kevin Broady of Gardner Lithograph; Brooks Roddan; Dianne Woo; and all of the photographers who contributed to this book.

Special thanks are due to Simon Johnston @ praxis: and Paul Kranhold at The Irvine Company.

Photographs are reproduced courtesy of the creators and lenders of the material depicted.

PHOTO CREDITS

FRONT MATTER
1   Stephen Francis
3   Stephen Francis
4   Stephen Francis
6   Lonnie Duka

INTRODUCTION
12   Ansel Adams, contemporary print from original negative, courtesy of UCR/California Museum of Photography, Sweeney/Rubin Ansel Adams FIAT LUX Collection, University of California, Riverside
13   (Top) Eric Figge
     (Bottom) Tom Lamb
14-15   Stephen Francis
16   Courtesy of Piedmont Pacific Trade Corporation
17   Photographer unknown, Courtesy of the LOS ANGELES TIMES

MASTER PLAN
18   Ansel Adams, contemporary print from original negative, courtesy of UCR/California Museum of Photography, Sweeney/Rubin Ansel Adams FIAT LUX Collection, University of California, Riverside
19   Generated by The Irvine Company, courtesy of The Irvine Company

HISTORY
22   Generated by The Irvine Company, courtesy of The Irvine Company
24   Photographer unknown, courtesy of The Irvine Company
25   Photographer unknown, courtesy of the Historical Library, First American Corporation
26-27   Photographer unknown, courtesy of The Irvine Company
28   Photographer unknown, courtesy of the Historical Library, First American Corporation
29   (Top and bottom) Photographer unknown, courtesy of the Historical Library, First American Corporation
30   Photographer unknown, courtesy of The Irvine Company
31   Photographer unknown, courtesy of the Historical Library, First American Corporation
32   Photographer unknown, courtesy of the Historical Library, First American Corporation
33   Photographer unknown, courtesy of the Historical Library, First American Corporation
34   Photographer unknown, courtesy of The Irvine Company
35   Photographer unknown, courtesy of The Irvine Company
36   Photographer unknown, courtesy of The Irvine Company
37   Courtesy of Gordon T. McClelland
38–39   Courtesy of Gordon T. McClelland
40   Photographer unknown, courtesy of the Historical Library, First American Corporation
41   (Bottom left) Book 1, page 13, photo P010219, UCI Chancellor's Campus Photograph Albums, 1959–1969, the University Archives, UC Irvine Libraries
     (Bottom right) Photographer unknown, courtesy of the Historical Library, First American Corporation
42–43   Photographer unknown, courtesy of the Historical Library, First American Corporation
44–45   Stephen Francis

LEISURE
48   John Connell
50   John Connell
51   Tom Lamb
52-53   John Connell
54-55   John Connell
56   John Connell
57   Ellen Smith-Spotts
58-59   Eric Figge
60   John Connell
61   Phillip Channing
62-63   John Connell